Let's Go to
the Potty!

For every parent who is about to spend a lot more time in the bathroom than they ever imagined. You've got this. —A.J.

Let's Go to the Potty!

A Potty Training Book for Toddlers

Allison Jandu

Illustrations by Luke Scriven

CALLISTO PUBLISHING

Wow, look at you!
You have gotten so big!

**When you were a baby,
that diaper was just right.**

But diapers are no fun.
Nobody likes to be
wet and dirty!

Here–this will help.
Your very own potty!

Your potty might look like this.

Or like this.

Let's try it out.
Look! It's just your size!

How do you know when to sit on the potty?

Listen to your body!

When you feel a rumble
in your tummy, or you need to
squat or squirm, that's how
you know it's time to go.

Find your grown-up and ask for help.

Let's go to the potty!
Hurry, hurry!

**Take off that old diaper
and sit down.**

You might have to wait for the pee and poop to come out.

But you can have lots of fun while you sit.

You can read, play, or sing the Potty Song!

Let's go to the potty,
We need to go right now!
I listen to my body.
I'm such a big kid, wow!

Try your best to put all of your pee and poop into the potty!

(It's where it likes to be!)

Sometimes you sit and sit,
but nothing comes out.

Don't worry! That's okay!

And sometimes pee and poop can surprise you.

Accidents happen—you can try again next time.

The important thing is that you keep on trying until . . .

You did it!
Hooray!
Look at you go!

Wait! You're not done yet.

Your grown-up will help you wipe your bottom.

Don't forget to wash your hands.

Go out and tell the world!

You should be so proud!

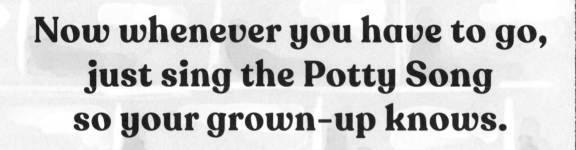

Now whenever you have to go,
just sing the Potty Song
so your grown-up knows.

Let's go to the potty,
We need to go right now!
I listen to my body.
I'm such a big kid, wow!

No more wet or dirty diapers for you.

You'll wear big-kid undies soon.

Your potty story is unique and special, just like you!

About the Author

Allison Jandu is a professional consultant who happens to love one of the milestones many parents dread the most: potty training. She thrives on helping children obtain their newfound pride and independence by learning to use the potty and leave the diapers behind.

Allison lives in Maryland and is a mom of two. In addition to *Let's Go to the Potty!*, she has written three highly praised potty training guides: *Potty Training for Busy Parents, The Poop Puzzle, and The Wee Hours.*

About the Illustrator

Luke Scriven is an illustrator/animator from South West England, where he lives with his fiancée and pet rabbit, who is an ongoing distraction from work! Luke specializes in children's illustration and is inspired by the likes of Tove Janson and Maurice Sendak. He uses watercolors, pens, and digital brushes to create his pictures and he is currently working on bringing his children's book, *A Little Fear*, to life.

Art Directors: Mando Daniel and Eric Pratt
Art Producer: Sue Bischofberger
Senior Editor: Sabrina Young
Associate Editor: Maxine Marshall
Production Editor: Jenna Dutton

Published by Callisto Publishing LLC C/O Sourcebooks LLC
P.O. Box 4410, Naperville, Illinois 60567-4410
(630) 961-3900
callistopublishing.com
This product conforms to all applicable CPSC and CPSIA standards.

Source of Production: Wing King Tong Paper Products Co. Ltd. Shenzhen, Guangdong Province, China
Date of Production: July 2023
Run Number: SBCAL28

Printed and bound in China.
WKT 29